The Pacific Ocean

By **Leighton Taylor**

Featuring the photographs of
Norbert Wu

BLACKBIRCH PRESS, INC.

WOODBRIDGE, CONNECTICUT

Published by Blackbirch Press, Inc.
260 Amity Road
Woodbridge, CT 06525

©1999 by Blackbirch Press, Inc.
First Edition

e-mail: staff@blackbirch.com
Web site: www.blackbirch.com

All photographs ©Norbert Wu/Mo Yung Productions except pages 3 (PhotoDisc); 6 (NASA)

Text ©Leighton Taylor

Printed in the United States

10 9 8 7 6 5 4 3 2

Editor's Note
The photos that appear on pages 20 (inset), 21 (inset), 32, and 43 (insets), show species that are found in the Pacific Ocean, but the photos were taken in a different locale. Because no suitable images of the species could be found in a Pacific Ocean environment, these very similar images were used instead.

Library of Congress Cataloging-in-Publication Data
Taylor, L.R. (Leighton R.)
The Pacific Ocean / by Leighton Taylor; photographs by Norbert Wu
    p.   cm. — (Life in the sea)
  Includes bibliographical references and index.
  Summary: In text and photographs, presents some of what is known about the Pacific Ocean, its islands, its people, and its exotic creatures.
    ISBN 1-56711-243-9 (library binding : alk. paper)
    1. Pacific Ocean—Juvenile literature. [1. Pacific Ocean.] I. Wu, Norbert, ill.
II. Title. III. Series: Taylor, L.R. (Leighton R.) Life in the sea
GC771.T38 1999
551.46'5—dc21   98-17329
                                                                    CIP
                                                                    AC

IMAGINE A VAST, GREEN OCEAN

Imagine an ocean so huge, that its waters run from the warm, sun-soaked beaches of South America to the frigid, aqua waters of Antarctica. Its waves crash upon the shores of California, Japan, Alaska, and Mexico as well. At its widest span, this vast ocean is 12,000 miles (19,300 kilometers) wide, nearly half the planet. Miles below the waves are some of the earth's deepest canyons and craters, filled with sea life that has never seen the light of a single day.

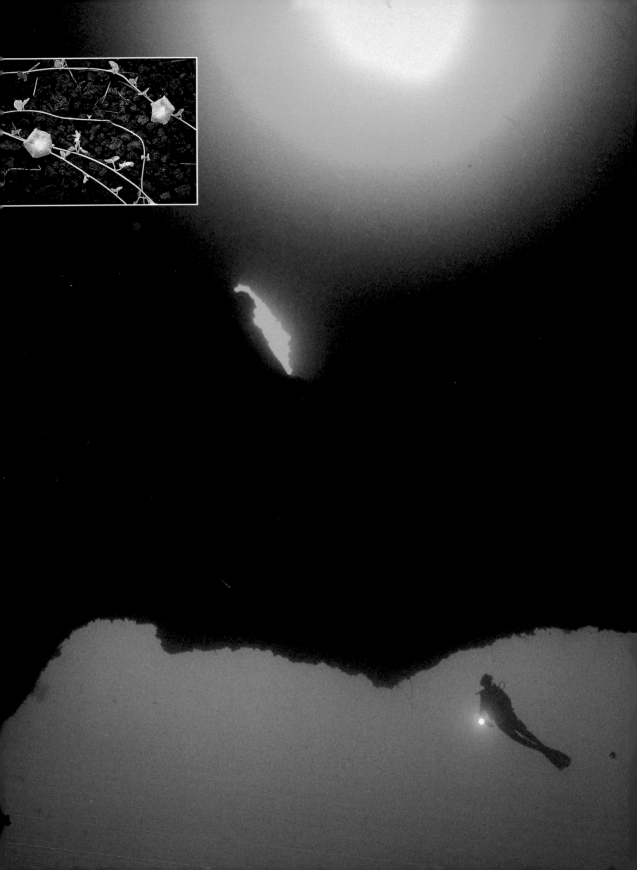

THE GREATEST OF OCEANS

You don't have to imagine! The Pacific Ocean is such a place. The Pacific Ocean is the largest, oldest, and deepest of the world's four big oceans.

All around the Pacific Ocean are volcanoes. Some of them are underwater. Some are on land. There are volcanoes in Japan, Alaska, California, Mexico, South America, Antarctica, and the Philippines. Scientists call the volcanic circle around the Pacific "The Ring of Fire." Lots of earthquakes happen around this ring, too.

The greatest depth on Earth is in the Pacific Ocean. It is called Challenger Deep, near the Philippine Islands. From the sunlit surface to the dark, dark bottom it's more than 5 miles (8 kilometers) down. The Pacific Ocean has icebergs and coral reefs. It has penguins and crocodiles. It has jellyfish and whales. It is so vast, it cannot all be covered in one short book.

In this book we will just talk about one big part of this great ocean—a large warm area near the equator in the Pacific. This region includes places called Micronesia and Polynesia. *Micronesia* means "tiny islands." *Polynesia* means "many islands." The islands of Micronesia are in the middle of the Pacific Ocean, known also as the South Pacific. The sun shines almost all the time. The islands are made by corals and volcanoes. The water is warm and filled with wonderful animals.

Opposite: **A diver approaches a dramatic spot where a hole in the coral reef opens to the sunlight above.** *Inset:* **Morning glories grow on volcanic rock, which makes up many islands in the Pacific.** *Right:* **A Pacific coral reef and tropical island.**

THE NATURE OF THE OCEAN

When astronauts look at Earth from space, they see a planet mostly covered by water. Some people call our Earth "Planet Ocean." That's because it has much more ocean than dry land.

From space, the world's ocean looks the same all over. But it can be very different from place to place. The water can be different. The location and shape of the holes filled by seawater can be special.

How is seawater different from one place to another? Here are three important ways that seawater can change, depending on:

1. how warm or cold it is
2. how much salt it holds
3. how clear or murky it is

Sea water in the area of Micronesia flows in complicated patterns called currents. Some currents are warmer and saltier than others. Some currents are on the surface. Some are deep.

El Niño is a famous warm current that forms every few years. Very warm water from areas near Micronesia flow near the equator toward North and South America. The warm water meets the coasts there and flows up and down the shores. Because it is so much warmer than the sea water that usually flows there, the current actually changes the weather. Much more rain falls in California for example, and places like Australia and Hawaii have long dry spells. Animals more common in Micronesia waters visit the coasts of California with the warm water. Manta rays, tunas, and other tropical fish like mahimahi surprise California fishermen during these times.

Oceanographers are scientists who study the ocean. They are very interested in learning more about El Niño and other currents. Oceanographers can tell a lot about the currents in the Pacific Ocean by using satellites. Cameras and instruments on satellites record the temperature, movement, and level of the ocean currents on the surface of the sea. Oceanographers also use ships to take water temperatures and measure ocean saltiness below the surface.

The limestone islands of Palau have been cut into strange but beautiful shapes by the ocean's water.

MORE THAN SEVEN SEAS—THE MANY WATERS OF THE WORLD

The location and shape of a basin filled by seawater gives each body of water special characteristics. The earth's seawater fits into holes of many different sizes and shapes. These giant holes are shaped by the land around them. The names for these different areas of seawater depend on their size and shape.

An *ocean* is the biggest area of seawater. An *ocean* is so big, it touches several continents. It can take many days to cross an ocean, even in a fast boat. The Pacific Ocean is the world's largest ocean. The Atlantic Ocean and the Indian Ocean are very large, too.

A *sea* is smaller than an ocean but still very big. A sea is more enclosed by land than an ocean and may touch only a few countries or even be in the middle of a single country. Sailing the "Seven Seas" is an old sailor's term. In reality, there are many more seas than seven. The Mediterranean Sea is a big, famous sea. It is connected to the Red Sea by the Suez Canal. The Caribbean Sea touches Florida and Mexico and has many islands.

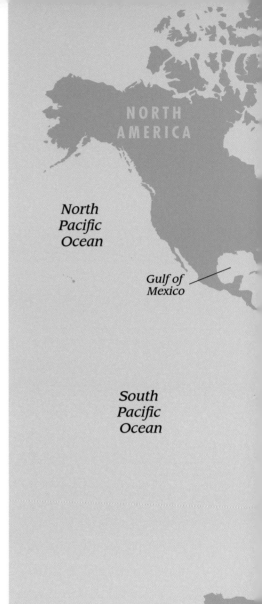

NORTH AMERICA

North Pacific Ocean

Gulf of Mexico

South Pacific Ocean

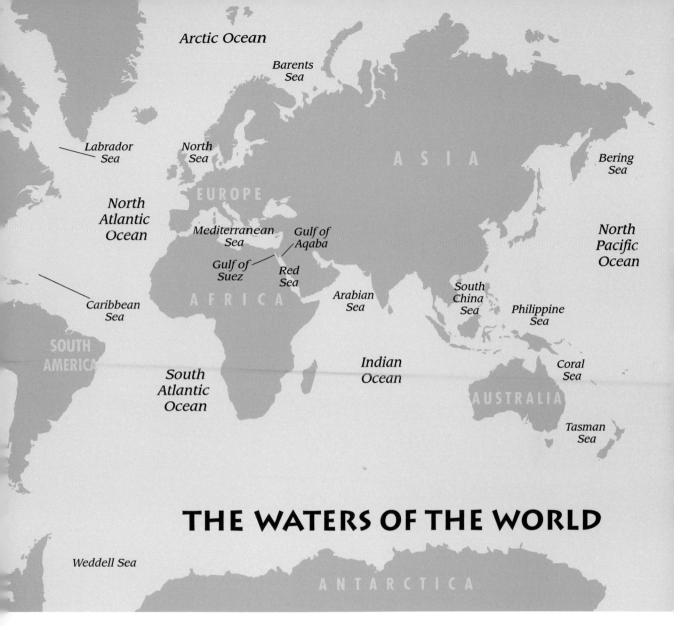

THE WATERS OF THE WORLD

Smaller parts of the ocean can be called a *gulf*. Sometimes gulfs are big, sometimes small. The Gulf of Mexico is very big. The Gulf of Aqaba (AH-ka-ba) and the Gulf of Suez are small. These gulfs are at the very top of the Red Sea.

MICRONESIA

There are many islands in Micronesia—some of them are quite large. Some Micronesian islands are made by volcanoes. Others are made of the hard parts of billions and billions of sea animals and plants.

The islands of Micronesia have different shapes, too. Some are high mountains with jungles. Some are low and flat. Some have airports, big buildings, and miles of highways. Other are barely big enough to hold a grass shack. From an airplane, some lagoons look like rings of coral beach with a big island of sea water in the middle. This kind of round island is called an atoll (AT-OLE) Almost all of the islands have coral reefs growing around them.

The many islands of Micronesia are spread over thousands of miles of the Pacific Ocean near the equator. Groups of islands are organized into separate countries. Some of them are the Federated States of Micronesia, the Republic of Palau, and the Marianas islands. All of them have close friendships with the United States. Most Micronesian people speak English.

The shallow lagoon in the middle of this atoll was formed over the sunken cone of an ancient volcano.

Inset top: A Tinker's butterflyfish is just one of many brilliantly colored animals that live in the warm waters of the Pacific.

Inset bottom: Some Pacific islands, such as this one, are barely big enough to house a large tree.

◄ **Huge coral reefs create a colorful underwater environment in the Pacific.**

ISLANDS MADE OF STONE

Many of the islands in the Pacific are atolls. All of the rocks and sand on an atoll have been made by animals and plants that lived on the nearby reefs. The special rock that sea animals and plants make is called "limestone." Reef creatures that make limestone—sea urchins, coral, snails, and clams—live on reefs in shallow water where there is plenty of sun.

A reef animal or plant needs some place to attach or crawl around. How do atolls get built in the middle of the ocean in deep water? More than 150 years ago, the famous biologist Charles Darwin explained the growth of an atoll: Long ago, on the sea bottom, in very deep water, a volcano erupted and pumped out a tremendous flow of hot rock called lava. There was so much lava that it stood above the level of the sea. The lava cooled and formed a new rocky island. Even today islands are still being made by volcanoes.

Soon, corals and other animals began to grow on the new rocks. The big pile of lava was so heavy that it gradually sank. As the island sank, the coral and other limestone builders kept growing. They grew on top of old dead skeletons of other animals and plants. The island kept sinking, but the reef kept growing. After millions of years, there was no lava rock to be seen. Only the skeletons of reef animals were left. Of course the top layer of the reef was still alive and growing.

Darwin had suggested a good way to prove this theory: Use a big drill to drill through the limestone of an atoll. In Darwin's day there were no drills big enough for such a job. He said to keep drilling until the drill hit lava rock. In the 1950s, scientists drilled such a hole on an island in Micronesia. They had to drill almost half a mile before they found lava, but they proved Darwin was right!

Left: **Lettuce coral covers the ocean bottom.**
Below: **Various species of soft corals create a brilliantly colored landscape in the Solomon Islands.**

JUST WHAT IS A CORAL, ANYWAY?

The strong branches of a coral head are built by thousands and thousands of tiny animals. There are many different kinds of corals. But each tiny animal is about the size of a pinhead. Some are as big as a pea. They look a lot like their bigger relatives, the sea anemones (A-NEM-O-NEES). Each coral animal is called a polyp (PAH-LIP). A polyp has a soft, circle-shaped body. Its mouth is in the center of the circle. Around the circle are long, soft bumps. The long bumps are called tentacles.

Tentacles are covered with very, very small poison cells. Corals use these poison cells to catch food. They also use them to keep enemies away. Each cell contains a coiled up dart or arrow and is filled with poison. When a small food animal or an enemy touches a tentacle, the poison cells burst open. The darts uncoil and fly out. They stab an enemy and inject poison.

Top: **The individual polyps of the star coral.** *Right:* **The individual stinging polyps can be seen on this soft coral tree.**

When a human touches a coral, the poison cells can cause a painful red rash.

Every polyp helps to build the coral skeleton. Polyps are soft—almost jelly-like—but they can build very hard skeletons around them. Coral skeletons can grow very big. They help form coral reefs. Over centuries, coral reefs can grow to become hundreds of miles long. These tiny animals can build big islands. Most of the islands in Micronesia were made by corals.

Top: **The flowery polyps of a plate coral.**
Middle: **A crab walks across the brightly colored polyps of a soft coral.**
Bottom: **The polyps of the leather coral look like tiny trees.**

CORAL COUSINS AND "GUESTS"

There are many kinds of animals that have poison cells, and soft circular bodies with mouths at the center. All of these animals are related to corals. They include jellyfish, sea anemones, sea fans, soft corals, and fire corals. Some of them build special skeletons. Black corals and sea fans build softer corals than reef corals but they are still strong. Black corals and pink corals are hard enough to be polished into valuable jewelry. Other coral relatives, such as sea anemones and jellyfish, don't make skeletons. Instead they have soft, jelly-like bodies.

Corals and some of their relatives are attached to the bottom and spend their lives in one place. But others can swim and drift around. Jellyfish live freely and can swim and drift for long distances. They can rest on the bottom. They can float on the surface.

Most coral animals and their relatives have special guests living in their bodies. These "guests" are tiny, one-celled plants. The plants make food that helps feed the coral animal. The plants also help corals and their relatives to take salts out of the water and make hard skeletons with them. All plants—including the guests of corals and their relatives—need sunlight. The coral animals that have these special plant guests need to stay in sunny, clear, warm water. The Pacific has plenty of that, so plenty of coral and their relatives live there.

Clown anemonefish rest amid the safety of the stinging tentacles of a host anemone.
Inset left: **Two longnose hawkfish swim between the polyps of a soft coral tree.**
Inset right: **Sea fans are relatives of corals.**

A LAKE FULL OF JELLIES

The Micronesian islands of Palau (PAL-OW—also called Belau) are surrounded by ocean. But in the middle of some of the larger islands there are lakes filled with salty water. People hike to these lakes through forests of bushes and trees that have poison spines. It's worth the hard hike, though. In these waters lives a special kind of jellyfish. Some small lakes can hold thousands of these eerie-looking creatures.

Each jellyfish has tiny helper plant cells living inside it. The plant cells use sunlight to make food, which the jellyfish shares. Because they don't have to hunt, the jellyfish have weak poison cells. People can swim in swarms of these jellyfish without getting stung. Great clouds of jellyfish swim across the lake every day. They stay in the places where the sun is brightest because sunlight helps their plant guests make food.

The jellyfish of certain lakes in Palau are harmless because their stinging cells are weak.

LIFE IS HARD—AND SALTY

What makes the ocean salty? The ocean is salty because of the many kinds of things that dissolve in it.

Sea water has a lot of salt dissolved in it. It also has all kinds of other elements in smaller amounts, such as gold, aluminum, copper, and something that is a lot like cement.

Corals take dissolved limestone from the ocean's water and turn it into a hard cement-like substance.
Inset: **Lobsters are one of many animals that make "cement" from the ingredients in sea water.**

◄ **Sea fans and other corals take limestone from the water and create the reef's "cement."**
Inset: **Crabs—like lobsters, snails, and sea stars—are good at making hard shells.**

This "cement" has several names, but "limestone" is a good one. The cement-like material that is dissolved in sea water is very important to most plants and animals on coral reefs. Corals are especially good at making dissolved limestone into hard stuff. So are some plants. So are snails, lobsters, crabs, sea stars, and sea urchins.

Reef animals and plants are so good at making limestone that they build whole islands out of it.

Tropical beach sand is made of the ground-up limestone skeletons of plants and animals. If you look closely at the sand, you can actually see parts of reef animals.

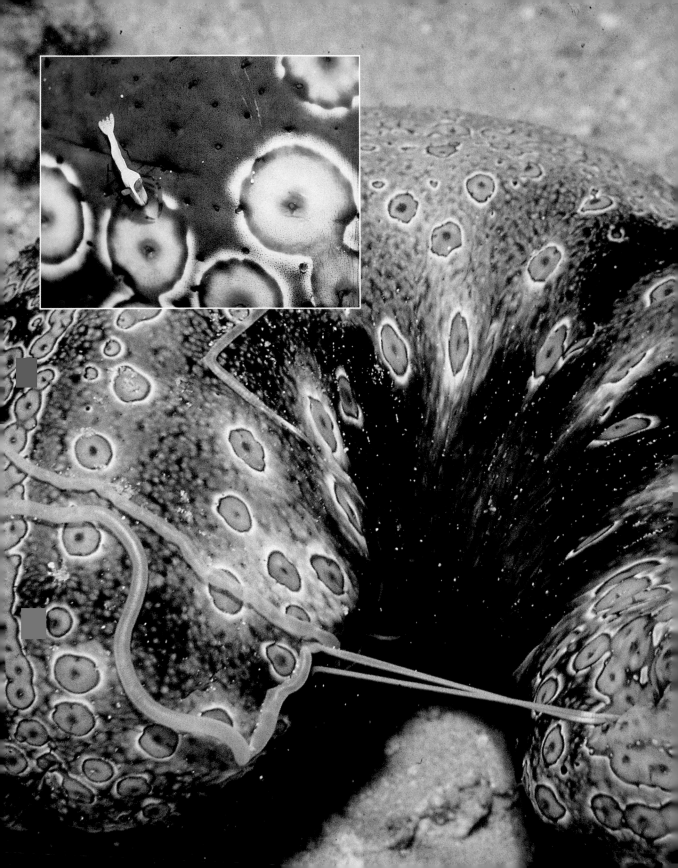

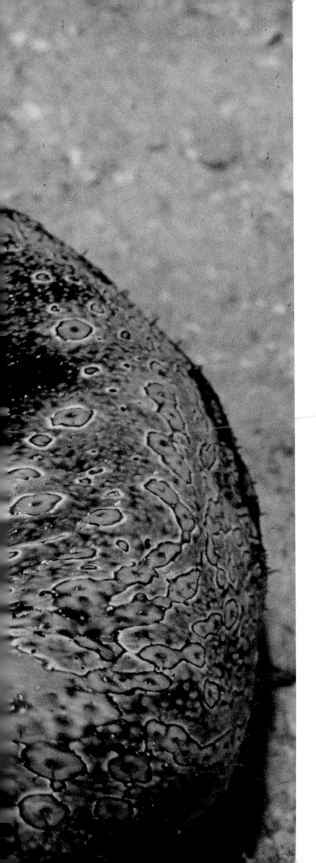

CUTE-SEA CUKES

Cucumbers grow on coral reefs, but they're not the kind you put in your salad! Sea cucumbers are animals shaped so much like green cucumbers that they were named after the vegetable. Even though they have a very different shape, sea cucumbers are close relatives of sea stars, sea urchins, and brittle stars.

Sea cucumbers chew sand. Tiny animals and chemicals in the sand are food for sea cucumbers. After they suck the food from the sand, sea cucumbers poop the sand out. Their poop looks like little crayon-sized sausages made of sand.

Although few people would put sea cucumbers in their salad, many people in Asia eat them. Dried sea cucumber (called trepang) makes tasty soup.

Sea cucumbers live on sandy and muddy bottoms all over the ocean. They are easy to see in the sunny waters on Micronesian reefs. But they also live in the deepest, darkest parts of the ocean.

Sea cucumbers get their food from eating sand.
Inset: **This close-up shows an emperor shrimp, which lives on the surface of a sea cucumber's skin.**

◀ **Longnose hawkfish use their snouts to grab food deep inside corals.**

NOSY FISH

Sometimes animals that look similar are close relatives. For example, African elephants (with very big ears) are close cousins to Indian elephants (with much smaller ears).

But sometimes animals that look a lot alike are not related at all. Pacific reefs are home to different kinds of fish with long noses (but no ears!). These fish are not closely related, yet they all have long noses or snouts to help them catch food.

Colorful filefish use their long snouts to snap up tiny crabs and other small creatures.

Longnose butterflyfish stick their noses far back in cracks to pluck out tiny crabs and worms. Longnose filefish use their snouts to reach into corals and grab single polyps. Longnose hawkfish live on sea fans and black coral. Their long snouts pluck crabs from the wiry branches of their homes.

The snout of the longnose butterflyfish is ideal for grabbing tiny crabs and worms from the reef's thin cracks and crevices.

A PEEK AT PUFFERS

Almost all fish have scales. Most scales look like tiny soft fingernails. They come off easily when a fish is injured or caught. But some fish have very special scales. Spiny pufferfish have scales that are long, hard spines. When a spiny puffer is calm and cruising, its spines lie down flat against its skin. When it is frightened, it swallows a lot of water and puffs up into a ball. This makes its spines stick out. When it's all puffed out, it is hard for a big fish or shark to bite the puffer. When puffers puff up inside a crack or hole in the reef, their spines help them wedge themselves tightly for protection.

Most scales—like these on a parrotfish—are like soft, flexible fingernails. *Inset left:* **The scales that cover this guineafowl puffer are soft and flexible.** *Inset right:* **The scales that cover this spiny porcupinefish are long and hard and are an effective defense.**

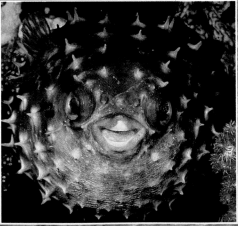

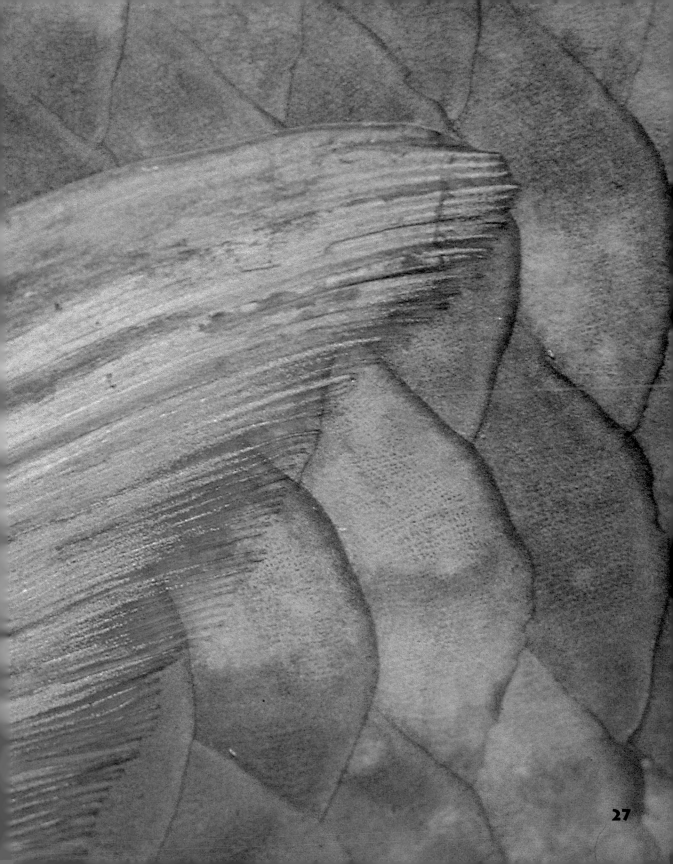

FATAL FISH

Lots of animals on the reef besides corals and their relatives make poison and use it as a defense. Some of the strongest poisons are made by fish. A few of these poisons are strong enough to kill people. Many of the most dangerous fish use sharp spines that inject poison like a doctor's needle injects medicine.

Poisonous fish often do one of two things—"show off" or lay low. The beautiful lionfish has big showy fins and bright red, brown, and black stripes. It is easy to see. The lionfish's markings

are a visual warning label—they're telling other reef animals (and divers) to "stay away!"

The stonefish hides by looking a lot like a bumpy rock or stone. Stonefish have the strongest poison of all fish. People have died by accidentally stepping on the spines of a stonefish.

Just as on land, some snakes in the ocean are equipped with poisonous defenses. Many different species of snake can be found in the waters of the world's warm oceans. The deadly banded sea snake is the most dangerous of all venomous snakes on earth. Its poison is an extremely powerful and effective killer, but it rarely bites humans.

Opposite: **A diver holds a deadly banded sea snake.**
Top: **The lionfish has a showy appearance that warns others to stay away.**
Middle and bottom: **Stonefish are some of the ocean's best camouflage artists—and the ocean's deadliest fish.**

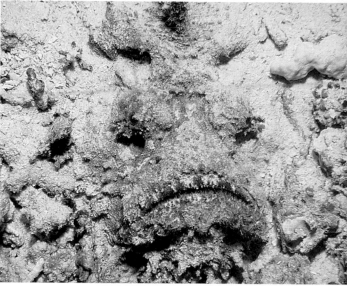

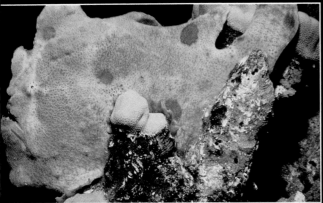

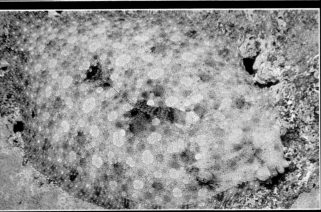

Top: **The mottled coloring of the crocodilefish makes it hard to see in the reef.**
Middle: **When it is still, a frogfish looks exactly like a sponge.**
Bottom: **Lying flat on the ocean floor, a flounder can make itself nearly invisible to enemies or prey.**

SOMETHING TO HIDE

Defenses and survival take on many forms in the natural world. Animals with strong poisons, sharp teeth, or dangerous spines have powerful weapons against attack. But many animals are not equipped with such powerful means of defense. Their best defense is to avoid trouble wherever possible—and that means avoid being seen in the first place!

Being able to blend into the surroundings is called camouflage. Some animals, such as the "spongy"-looking frogfish or the seaweed-like pipefish, have a kind of "natural" camouflage that comes from the way their bodies and colors blend with their habitat. Other animals have to work at camouflage a bit more. The thin, flat flounder, for example, can actually change its color to match the surroundings as it lies flat and motionless on the ocean floor.

Top: Although the colorful butterfly fish is easy to see, its markings hide its true intentions—its eyespots make it look as if it's moving in one direction, when it is really moving the opposite way.

Above: The protusions on a scorpionfish's face make it look just like a coral-covered rock.

Right: The body of a pipefish can easily be mistaken for a piece of seaweed.

SHELLING OUT

All crabs make hard shells from the limestone-like chemicals dissolved in sea water. This strong cover protects them. It covers every part of their body, even their eyes. This hard cover is also a skeleton that helps their muscles work.

A hermit crab makes itself a home inside an empty shell.

◀ **A spider crab creeps along the feathery branches of an urchin-like creature called a crinoid.**

Humans have skeletons that are underneath our muscles. Crabs have skeletons and shells that are outside their bodies. As a crab grows bigger, it must get a bigger skeleton. When you grow, your clothes may not fit you anymore. So you get bigger clothes. The crab does the same thing, but it makes its own covering. It crawls out of its old, smaller crab shell. Right after it crawls out, its shell is soft. Crabs with their fresh new cover are called "soft-shelled" crabs.

Very soon the new shells harden and become strong skeletons. Some crabs get extra protection by using the shells of dead snails and other animals. Hermit crabs, for example, use sea snail shells.

GENTLE GIANTS, OR CLAMMY KILLERS?

Many kinds of clams grow on Pacific reefs. But the most famous kind is the giant clam. Baby giant clams are only as big as your thumbnail. After many years, however, this baby clam grows to a very large size—bigger than a kitchen sink! Full-grown, the two shells of a giant clam would make bathtubs for twin human babies!

Like all clams, these giants have a big muscle that pulls the two shells together or opens them. This muscle tastes very good to many people. But being a favorite food of humans often means problems for an animal. People have been killing too many giant clams. They can't grow fast enough on the reefs and are becoming rare.

Giant clams have tiny helper plants living in their bodies that help the clams to grow. The plants need sun. Clams have simple eyes that sense the sunlight. The clams make sure the plants get plenty of sunlight.

Old legends told of clams that closed quickly and trapped divers by holding their hand tightly. It was said that divers drowned while being held under by giant clams. That's how they got the nickname "killer clams." These legends aren't true. Clams close very slowly and are usually found only in shallow water.

The mantle of a giant clam contains simple "eyes" that are sensitive to light.
Opposite: **A diver takes a look down inside the shell of a giant clam.**

A SURE-FOOTED SUCKER

All these animals are related: sea stars, brittlestars, sea urchins, and sea cucumbers. They come in different shapes, sizes, and colors. Some have big spines, some have little spines or smooth skin. But they all have many "feet" that look like tiny suction cups. Of course, these aren't feet like we have, but they do use them to move around on the reef, sand, and rocks. These sucking feet are called "tube feet" because they are shaped like tiny tubes with suckers on them.

Sea stars and their relatives move by holding on with some sucking feet while others let go. Some sea stars eat clams. The clam closes its shell tightly for protection, but the sea star uses its many sucking feet to pull the clam apart. When it pulls the shells open just a little way, the sea star pushes its own stomach out of its mouth and inside the clam. The stomach digests the clam's body inside the clam's own shells. Then the sea star pulls its stomach back into itself and moves along on its sucking feet to find another clam or animal it can eat.

A brittle sea star moves its long tentacles over a sea fan.
Inset top: A sea star rests on a soft coral tree.
Inset bottom: The crown of thorns sea star.

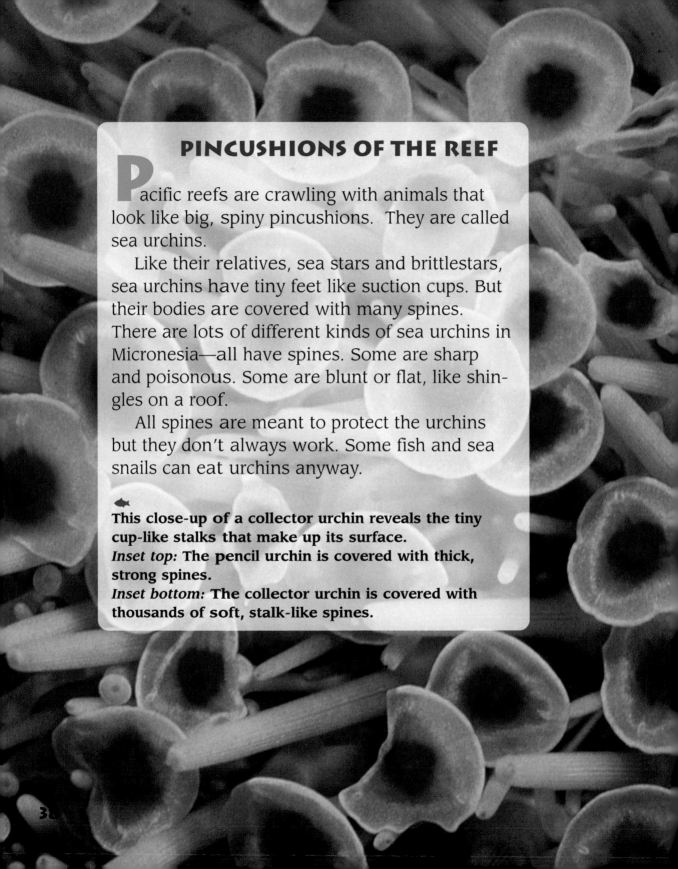

PINCUSHIONS OF THE REEF

Pacific reefs are crawling with animals that look like big, spiny pincushions. They are called sea urchins.

Like their relatives, sea stars and brittlestars, sea urchins have tiny feet like suction cups. But their bodies are covered with many spines. There are lots of different kinds of sea urchins in Micronesia—all have spines. Some are sharp and poisonous. Some are blunt or flat, like shingles on a roof.

All spines are meant to protect the urchins but they don't always work. Some fish and sea snails can eat urchins anyway.

This close-up of a collector urchin reveals the tiny cup-like stalks that make up its surface.
Inset top: **The pencil urchin is covered with thick, strong spines.**
Inset bottom: **The collector urchin is covered with thousands of soft, stalk-like spines.**

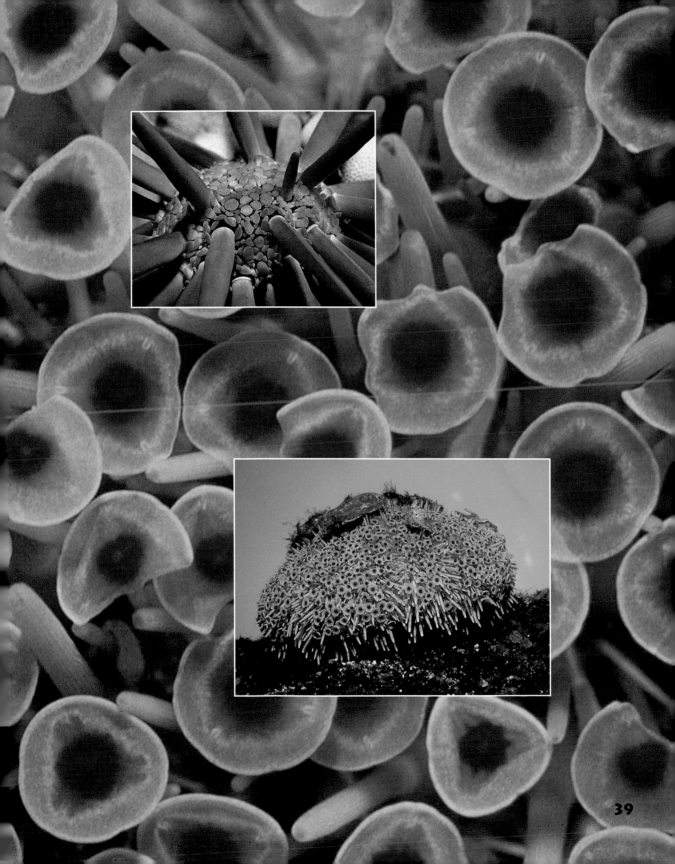

LIFE HIDDEN IN THE SAND

Divers and snorkelers in the warm Pacific—particularly in Micronesia—pay close attention to the exciting coral reefs. There are many fish there and lots of colorful sea fans, sponges, and corals. The sandy bottoms around the reefs may at first look boring and empty. But the sand is an exciting and interesting place—if you just look carefully.

Many kinds of animals live in the sand—at least part of the time—even fish. Garden eels live there all the time. Small wrasses bury themselves in the sand when they "sleep." Goatfish cruise the sand feeling around for food with their barbels.

A goby and a blind shrimp work together to clean their burrow in the sand.

Inset opposite below: Eels like this blue ribbon eel often bury themselves up to their heads in the sand.

Inset opposite top: This pair of fire gobies are just two of many species that make their home on the ocean bottom.

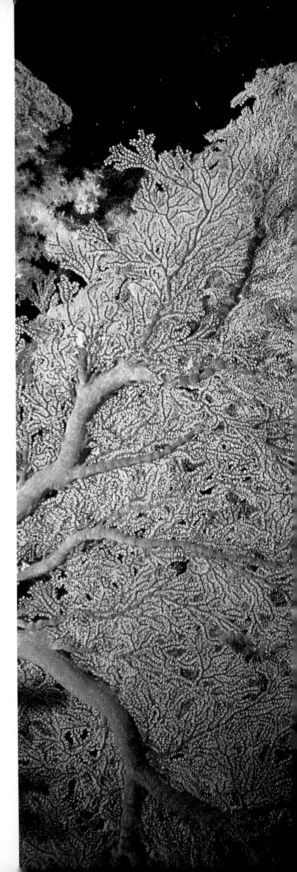

NAUTILUS

Many special animals live in the warm waters of the Pacific. One of the most interesting lives in deep water at the base of the steep walls of coral reefs. This animal has a shell, but it's not a clam. It has eyes but it's not a fish. It has strong soft legs but it's not a squid. It is, however, related to squid and octopus. This special animal is called the nautilus.

Nautilus have round brown and white shells as big as a dinner plate. Inside, the shell is divided into waterproof sections. The shell helps the nautilus float.

Octopus have eight legs, squid have ten. Nautilus have more than twenty legs. They also have a beak in their mouths. They use their beaks to crunch shrimp and crabs. Like the squid and octopus, chambered nautilus lay eggs. When the eggs are ready, tiny nautilus the size of a coin hatch out of each egg.

A nautilus floats freely in front of a coral wall.
Inset top: **This foot-long cuttlefish is a relative of the squid and nautilus.**
Inset bottom: **The octopus is a larger, shell-less nautilus relative.**

NAN MADOL, CITY OF MYSTERY

Old-time houses in Micronesia were built on land from small stones and tree trunks. Most often, palm leaves were used for roofs. Today, Micronesian houses look a lot like the old ones but they are made of concrete blocks with metal roofs.

Perhaps no modern building is as exciting as the structures that were built in the mysterious city of Nan Madol. Nan Madol is on the island of Ponape, one of the countries of Micronesia. All that remains of this ancient city of buildings are the giant, long rocks that were used to build it. These huge rocks look like gigantic logs. The "logs" are made from stone that came from some far away place. People had to bring these very heavy, long rocks on boats they paddled and sailed. No one is sure exactly how they did it, or how they built the buildings.

The city of Nan Madol was not built on land. It stood in shallow water. To get from one building to another, people must have used small boats. We don't know very much about the people who built Nan Madol hundreds of years ago. But they must have been excellent builders to lift such heavy rocks.

APPENDIX A:
HOW DO YOU MAP AN OCEAN?

A taxi driver can find an address by using a map and street signs. But how can a sailor find a location on the broad, empty ocean? When a boat sails near land, sailors can recognize landmarks. A map, or even a drawing of mountains and cliffs and beaches, can help them find their way. Some of the first maps made by sailors were made on the Red Sea. We know that the Egyptian Queen Hatshepsut sailed the length of the Red Sea about 2,500 years ago.

But in the open sea, away from land, there aren't any signs. And how can you make a map of a place that is all ocean?

Here's how: All mapmakers have agreed on two kinds of imaginary lines that cover the earth. One set of lines go from the top of the earth—at the North Pole—to the bottom of the earth—at the South Pole. These are the lines of "longitude" (lonj-EH-tood). The other lines go around the earth from east to west. These are the lines of "latitude" (lat-EH-tood). The latitude line that goes around the fattest part of the earth (at its middle) is the called the equator. Above the equator is the Northern half of the earth, also known as the Northern Hemisphere. Below the equator is the Southern part of the earth. That's the Southern Hemisphere.

The equator is easy to find on a globe. But mapmakers also divide the earth in half going north to south. This line divides the world into two halves, too—the western half and the eastern half. Every line is numbered with degrees as they move around the circular earth.

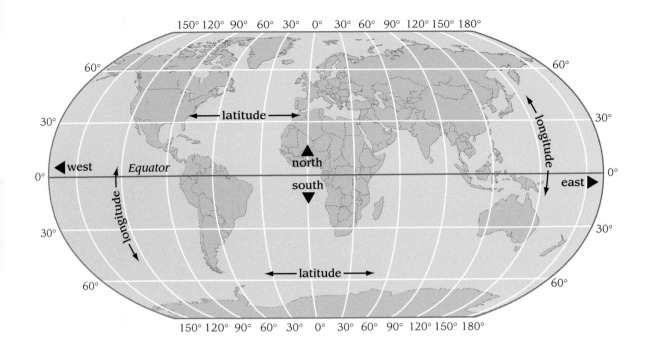

You can find places in the Pacific Ocean on a map of the world by using "positions." A position is the place where a particular place on the latitude and a particular place on the longitude meet.

To find the North Pacific off the coast of California, first find the longitude line for 135 degrees west. Find the latitude line for 35 degrees north. The two lines will cross in the North Pacific Ocean.

But such lines only appear on maps. Nobody can actually draw them on the ocean! So how do sailors find their positions? By looking at the sky! At any given time, the moon, stars, and the sun are in predictable places. If a navigator knows what time it is and can measure the location of the sun, moon, or a few stars, he or she can find a position on Earth.

A new and even easier way has recently been invented. Navigators can use small computers that use satellites instead of stars to find a position of latitude and longitude.

GLOSSARY

atoll A special kind of island made by coral reefs.

current A small or large body of water that is moving slower or faster than the water around it.

Equator The imaginary line of latitude that goes around the waist of the Earth (from east to west).

gulf A large part of an ocean or sea that reaches into the land.

latitude Imaginary lines that go around the earth from east to west (side to side). Map makers draw them on maps to show where places are located.

limestone A fairly soft, white rock. Chalk, seashells, corals, and cement all contain limestone.

longitude Imaginary lines that go around the earth from north to south (up to down). Map makers draw them on maps to show where places are located.

navigation Finding where you are (your **position**) by using mathematics, time, stars, and maps.

oceanographer A scientist who studies the ocean and seas— including their currents, waves, plants and animals.

polyp One tiny coral animal. Many coral polyps make up a coral colony, or group.

position The exact place where someone or something is, described as a point where a specific latitude and specific longitude meet.

FURTHER READING

Bramwell, Martyn. *The Oceans* (Earth Science Library). Danbury, CT: Franklin Watts, Inc., 1994.

Clarke, Penny. *Beneath the Oceans* (Worldwise series). Danbury, CT: Franklin Watts, Inc., 1997.

Lambert, David. *The Pacific Ocean* (Seas and Oceans series). Chatham, NJ: Raintree/Steck-Vaughn, 1997.

Savage, Stephen. *Animals of the Oceans* (Animals by Habitat series). Chatham, NJ: Raintree/Steck-Vaughn, 1997.

INDEX